TWO SIDES OF AN ISLAND

TWO SIDES OF AN ISLAND
and Other Poems

BY

MARTIN HALPERN

Chapel Hill
THE UNIVERSITY OF NORTH CAROLINA PRESS

CONTEMPORARY POETRY SERIES

Copyright © 1954, 1955, 1956, 1957, 1959, 1960, 1961, 1962, 1963
by Martin Halpern

Manufactured in the United States of America

Some of the poems in this collection have appeared in *Audience, Beloit Poetry Journal, Botteghe Oscure, Carleton Miscellany, Commentary, Hudson Review, Kenyon Review, Literary Review, Minnesota Review, Perspective, Quarterly Review of Literature, Voices,* and *Western Poet.*

PRINTED BY THE SEEMAN PRINTERY, DURHAM, N. C.

To Nancy

CONTENTS

I. VIEWS AND CONJECTURES

Two Sides of an Island	3
The Myopic Musician	4
The Euphoric Playwright	5
The Incomplete Angler	6
Occasions	7
My Mother's Father	8
Reflection in the Louvre	9
Departures from a Passage in Boethius	10
A Note for a Favorite Student	12
In Limited Defense of Reason	13
The Two Nevadas	14
Mussel and Caterpillar	16
Ishmael the Scrivener	17

II. FROM AN ITALIAN JOURNAL: 1956-57

The After-Dream	23
With a Camera in Taormina	25
Traffic Accident on the Via Nazionale	26
Tristano ed Isotta	27
Ode	28
The Trams of Rome	30
Roman Farewell	32
A Birthday Card to Myself	33

III. WEATHERS, WITHOUT AND WITHIN

Meditation on the Beach in Provincetown	37
Après le Déluge	39
Elegy During a Convalescence	40
The Lady and the Pilgrim	41
Sunshower	42
The Balloon	43
Late Afternoon Spring Sounds Beside Two Oceans	44
Summer Impromptu	45
After Hiking Up "Imp Face" Mountain	46
A Memento	47
On the Year's First Picnic	48
Rake's Song	50
Two Reflections for Nancy	51
The Osprey	53

I. VIEWS AND CONJECTURES

TWO SIDES OF AN ISLAND

Should the shore he depended on turn out rock, rounding
Tide-smoothed and slime-shellacked to drownable depth,
What spent swimmer would not, as he gasped
For the grant of breath to persist, gasp, too, at the sudden
Mereness of his humanity?

                          Loosed, heave
After heave of rebounding wave from his hand's brief holds
On the rock he cannot climb but at least would lean
And gasp against, what is his will now but
Bare frenzy for foothold, one sheer hope or habit
Short of the barest frenzy for absolution?

We differ in how close we have come to drowning:
Few, even in thought, closer than where the whelmed
Hand may first fail to bother reaching back.

So let a second wind reprieve him. Let
Reacting limbs splash penitence to their wake,
And before the grant give out, far leeshore sand
Responsive to clutch of clambering finger and foot
Accept his collapse. What then?

                                  Well, how many heroes
Who differ, we guess, in degree from us who project them,
Have gasped thus, gained that grant, and woken squinting,
Through yesterday's terror and dreams of a dismal Avernus,
Sunward—all humanly touched and tempted by
Some island maid's humane, betrayable eyes?

THE MYOPIC MUSICIAN

Unless the apple show teeth-marks, or the vase
The smudge of a half-patched crack where somebody once,
By temper, accident, or perverse design,
Placed some impression of himself, still-lifes
Don't fathom me, nor headless torsos minus
Due reference to the horror of headlessness.
The fleshliest pink of Rubens might as well
Be Fra Angelico blue, and either alike,
Imagined apart from the limbs and looks they distinguish,
Hue of concupiscence or chastity.
How chimes it then, that these unvouched vibrations,
Which cannot prophesy, define, nor x-ray
The least joint of the human complex, deal
Such largess to the mind it can forego
All zeal for prophecy or definition
Or solitude-divesting insight?

       Listen.
Bach on the phonograph: a fugue just ripened
To full ensemble. Released from the burden of meanings,
The mind unflexes, chooses one and one
Voice only to be its bearer while, unheeded
But heard, the rest attend coequally,
Till one or another succeed to the intimate center;
And so borne, dotes on the idealized likeness
Of its own constant but unsynchronized
Polyphony. Does such a grace of work
Bear it true tidings of the grace beyond
Works and the human complex, never trusted
To shape of stone or pattern of paint by vice
Of their very longevity? Is hearing, least
Possessive of senses, therefore the only sense
Eternity is safe to dally with?

A man may know this much: he hush-a-byes
His loudest lacks until that dalliance ends,
Swears up and down—and then forgets he swore—
That God must love him for his love of Bach.

THE EUPHORIC PLAYWRIGHT

As soon as I'd found them names, the play progressed.
It's just as well they weren't the best I could find:
A light switched on in a backstage room of my mind
Where anemic figures, struggling to adjust

To those names, as to ill-fitting costumes, got
Such stimulation from the exercise,
Fresh blood went pumping through their arteries,
And back, through cleansed and expanded veins, to their
    hearts.

So now they're all wrought up. Now to convert them
From sanguine novices to knowing adults;
Now so to plot their growings that, though built
Only of words, my sticks and stones may hurt them.

THE INCOMPLETE ANGLER

In two hours, fishing for flounder at full tide
Up the creek from Inspiration Point,
I caught twelve small, spiney, inedible bullheads,
Which added injury to disappointment,
Scratching the hand that unhooked them. "Time
Is but the stream I go a-fishing in."
Thoreau. All right, some catch flounder, some
Bullheads. And some must do as I did then:
Rearing back, arch the thirteenth and last bait
Beyond the clear deep center into the rocky
Far-shore shallows, where flounder may
Be scarcer but so are bullheads. A boy who'd been luckier
Yelled, "You're crazy mister," but the tug
Came large to the palm and larger the harder I reeled;
Till one yank left, in the invisible snag,
Hook, line, and sinker. "Maybe so," I yelled,
As, lightfooted, past the grinning boy, past shame,
I shouldered my ridiculous rod downstream.

OCCASIONS

You might say the devil's mouth is small:
He must divide to devour; his meat
Is a mess of members sinewed to no whole;
Or, more delectable yet,
The whole well bled to nourish one
Fatted part, which a twist
In the right joint breaks off clean.

                                            Whereas the man
Intact, the rich man prodigal of interest
But of principle tight, who composes contraries
In his spirit's rhythm as the skilled
Pianist plays fours against threes,
Can turn the devil's appetite cold.

You might ask, how can you say this? I can't,
Except on occasions when I am that man.

MY MOTHER'S FATHER

My mother's father, crippled and seventy,
Waited for death on the living room couch
And passed the time re-reading Spinoza.

That spring was coming he knew by the clamor
Of boys below in the street, and the bounce
Of their ball against pavement and building and headache.

Although a Jew, my mother's father
Preferred Spinoza to Talmud and Torah,
And would scoff at the sketch of a fidgety godhead

Who altered his plans with every report
That the chosen people were still disappointing
His faith in their sense of propriety.

The ball bounced in through the open window,
Skipped from the sill, and before he could budge,
Had bumped both glasses and book to the floor.

My mother's father, alone in the house,
Sick to his stomach and throbbing with headache,
Studied the blur of the ball in his lap.

He groped for his glasses but couldn't quite reach them,
And couldn't quite reach the Works of Spinoza,
Sprawled on their face by his crippled left leg.

And so he prayed. He closed his eyes and, silently,
To Yaveh, Lord of Abraham and Isaac, prayed
For "sense enough to place this minor accident,
This random crime, *sub specie aeternitatis.*"

REFLECTION IN THE LOUVRE

To make his John the Baptist decent,
Leonardo, it is said,
Straddled with fur his sexual precinct,
Set a funny fur hood on his head,

And changed the name to Bacchus. For
Someone'd complained, whose tastes were clean,
That, bodies being what they are,
A seer should be heard, not seen.

The staff he crooks was surely a cross
Until its horizontal beam
Got blent back into that wilderness—
The Tuscan one—from which it came.

Yet challenge, not mirth, stares out of his eyes;
The sober Hebrew scruples linger;
And nothing in that flip disguise
Can draw attention from the finger

Pointing off left at an event
Unmaskable as his nakedness:
A way prepared, a sent one sent. . . .
And still, a flesh redeemerless.

DEPARTURES FROM A PASSAGE IN BOETHIUS

"This is the difference," quod sche, "that tho thinges that I purposide the a litel herbyforn (that is to seyn, the sonne arysynge and the man walkynge), that therwhiles that thilke thinges ben idoon, they ne myghte nat ben indoon; natheles that oon of hem, or it was idoon, it byhovide by necessite that it was idoon, but nat that oothir. Ryght so is it here, that the thinges that God hath present withoute doute thei shollen be. But som of hem descendith of the nature of thinges (as the sonne arysynge); and som descendith of the power of the doeris (as the man walkynge). . . ."

Chaucer's Translation

1.

The sun doesn't rise of course; the earth goes down.
Yet both ways, one mile moved is always and only
One mile, come cloud or clear sky. For a man,
Though, one mile down a country road alone
Is much of a walk or little, according to how
Crowded his thinking, how many felt alterations
In weather or shape and color of tree, bush, flower,
What kinds of hills or curves or signs or houses
Parcel the minutes and steps to his destination.
A man steering a ship through a changeless ocean
Would never make it to port unless the knots
Were landmarked, inch by inch, by his mind's motions
Giving the lie to Zeno's paradox.

2.

While a student in Cambridge, I once grew half obsessed
By a pair of lean, mad, middle-aged twin brothers
I'd see morning on morning, just walking, quite fast,
Up and down Harvard Square and environs together.
Dressed spiffly alike, slouch hat to shining shoe,
Their thin gray eyes and sallow faces set
In a mask of impatience, up Mass. Avenue,
Down Boylston, Brattle, or Mount Auburn Street,
But seldom the same direction twice in a row,
They'd match long strides intent on destinations

That clearly weren't there. In times of self-pity,
They'd move through my mind as types of the human
    condition:
With nowhere to go, but in motion to know they existed.

3.

Later, in Rome, I watched once from the rear
Of the church of *Trinità dei Monti* five nuns
At their afternoon devotions. For close to an hour
The rapt hush held. Diagonal columns of sun
Filtered across what seemed, before a single
Unflickering candle ringed with white gladiolas,
Five parts of the architecture—five matched triangles,
Jet-black and marble-smooth. And then it was over:
Five rustling habits creased with time, five wimpled
Facial expressions, all different, ascended the aisle;
And one old face, as it passed, turned briefly to me
What looked like a sort of a half of a sly smile,
As if to say, "Quite a performance, eh?"

4.

The sun doesn't set; the earth just turns away.
Both ways, the event, as indifferent to the time
And space it exists in as they to it, may lie
Under and over what move us, but is not them.
In tonight's most tranquil twilight, love, when the sea
And sky seemed one, three gulls one part of the shore
They perched on, and we one part of shore, sea, sky,
Why did it solace but not suffice? We share
This earth's given revolvings while steering, whether
At motion or rest, through distances and weathers
Unsharably our own. And should one hour,
Mile, minute, or step precisely repeat any other,
How, love, would our love, and you and I, endure?

A NOTE FOR A FAVORITE STUDENT

Having, for some days, watched them at their being,
I have a point to make, concerning clouds.
They are not lonely. Nor serene. Nor fleeting
Except when wind-blown. They are not allowed

Moods, and their modes are untransposable.
They lie, like little but themselves, above
Actions replete with you and me, and still,
Except when wind-blown, they are never moved.

So should you speak of clouds, be noncommittal.
Slur them. Say, for example, four clouds were,
Upon a sky-blue sky, the vast and vital
Day I discovered Homer; date preferred.

Or, one monopolized the whole horizon
Most of this morning. Meanwhile, I was pained
With recollection at the rapid rising
Against it of a great black bomber plane.

To be a human being is to be
Alone in such things. Though we radiate
Ourselves, only our selves can more than seem
More than the vapors from which they are made.

IN LIMITED DEFENSE OF REASON

The solid line down the curving fogbound road
May lull to a mortal stupor, but that
Is the lesser risk. Blind nights like these, we need,
Foremost, distinctions. If the straight
Clear paint-strip dividing hither from thither lane
Be arbitrary as nothing in nature, yet
By the light of that line,
I passed my neighbor in safety and made it home tonight.

Country is cordial here: the smallest child
Secure on the gradual shore; no beasts in the wood,
Sharks in the waves, poisonous snakes in the field,
Hills one can't cross, road or no road, on foot.
And if tomorrow, wind from the right quarter
Restores to vision all the fog now buries,
I and my neighbor may draw from the landscape's disorder
Order sufficient to any secular terrors.

But tonight we are accommodated men,
Who, passing on that visibility-zero
Acute curve of a hill-road, each in his lane
Protected if estranged, drove on toward tomorrow
With natures yet ours to save. By grace of the line,
Seen sidelong, not with the lulling full fixed gaze,
My neighbor and I
Have made it home tonight in safety, if not in grace.

THE TWO NEVADAS

    So flat and unfeatured the late night driver
Can purge by enacting that too recurrent nightmare
Of racing ever after the same forever
Unreachable horizon, the westbound highway,
Flanked north and south by a hundred desert miles,
Bisects the abstract borderline that rules
    Off Utah's laws, and starts to bore
Into Nevada's black interior.

    Once, twice in an hour, at the point of mock
Infinity where converging roadsides meet,
Bright headlights from some oncoming auto or truck
Impinge on the mock-dream; then, the silent rite
Of the dimming of lights recalls him briefly to
The human communion—the modest, considerate bow
    Exchanged, acknowledged, understood,
And both tear on to a darker solitude.

    But mostly, intact the blackness he chases;
Till, harbingered by sky-glow, mirage-like at first
Then brightening to fact, the neon oasis
Blocks the pursuit as if conjured complete from the dust.
So, braking to town-speed, back of the flashing facades
He glimpses the famous, well-lit, uncurfewed bars,
    Dressed ranks of one-armed bandits, and, tightly
Ingathered from who knows where in the vacant night,

    Communers in this other Nevada—
Garden of legal grace in the puritan waste,
Where money and marriage are simply made and unmade,
Where living-as-gamble is ethos government-blessed,
And where, well blinded to distances beyond,
He well might call it a day, content to squander
    His unspent tensions lost in that mass
Fascination, mass-willed abandon of will to chance.

    But if, however tempted, the driver
Accelerate westward till clear of the sky-glow, say
It is some subtler species of gambler's fever
That hounds him after the night's unknown; and he

Must cover a couple of hundred unsettled miles
More of that first Nevada, to earn his will's
    Refreshment in a light not neon,
But of the ever gaining, certain sun.

MUSSEL AND CATERPILLAR

The mussel is a minder of its own business.
Tucked in a narrow coign of self-made shell,
Sand-fast or rock-fast it contrives to dwell—
Conservative conservor of its own Isness.

The caterpillar is a different story.
Feeder for future, mean means of Becoming,
With and like worms it crawls, but while so slumming,
Harbors the butterfly's potential glory.

One yet may rise; the other may be pearled.
There's more than one way to enrich a world.

ISHMAEL THE SCRIVENER

Round and around, then, and ever contracting towards the button-like black bubble at the axis of that slowly wheeling circle, like another Ixion did I revolve. Till gaining that vital centre, the black bubble upward burst; and now liberated by reason of its cunning spring, and, owing to its great buoyancy, rising with great force, the coffin lifebuoy shot lengthwise from the sea, fell over, and floated by my side.

Melville, Epilogue to *Moby Dick*

"Eh!—He's asleep, ain't he?"
"With kings and counselors," murmured I.

Melville, "Bartleby the Scrivener"

1.

I picture Ishmael recuperating—
Hail-fellow Ishmael, that jack of all fates
But mastered by none; inveterate voyeur,
Moralist, funny man, and self-styled orphan;
Amateur voyager over the storms of the mind's
Atlantic, voids of its Pacific, and
What polar wastes such sanity could sail in
And still return; exhausted, and well-met
By land after the fabulous fiasco,
His once clear comic vision scathed from looking
Too long and directly into the light of another's
Unfiltered madness. I picture his retreat.

2.

I see him moving inland, waiting for time
To work its routine cure. He'd watched the sea
Closing back in over the Pequod's plummet,
To roll on as it rolled five thousand years
Before that momentary whirlpool of waste
Perturbed its outer surface. What is most final,
Experience would assure him, will prove most
Supportable.

But he'd learn to learn, perhaps,
How some catastrophes can never relent;

« 17 »

How, out of their initial crash and concussion,
Will issue a chain of waneless echoes that neither
Divides at once to silence nor slowly blends
Into the old accustomed harmonies.
The farther he'd move from the sea, the more his anguish
Would come to dwell, not on the sea's own image
In stable magnitudes of mourning, but
On shallower rivers that wound round and around
Remembrance, roaring on turns over rapids which all
But annulled them, yet continuing; that, wanting
A gulf to complete their course, could only empty
Back on themselves their drift from the wreck's debris.

3.

While others were grinding axes to level at last
The fossil Tree of Guilt, or blazing to beat
All hell the advent of *Whim* as liberator
To man's old past-bound conscience, he, as wary
As they of the old tough answers, could not rest soft
On the grounds of their fall. The Letter of the Law
Was fading, jot by tittle, to leave a blank
White page as seal of the age's dispensation.
Yet guilt in the guise of his dead shipmates' shadows,
Unleveled, unliberated, undispensed,
Still massed in the way of his light; till he might have given
His own right leg to see where the rest of him stood,
Could he even dream the giving could promise the seeing.

Unable to laugh the past still, as he used to, or yield,
Like Ahab, to one imperfect but potent obsession,
He might, as his noblest dream, have willed himself
Curled in the shade of some thick high prison wall,
Dying for spite of hunger and reticence—
"To sleep," one mourner would announce, baffled
To homage by so pure a protest, "with kings
And counselors." Here, then, was the ultimate whim:
To say to existence, "I would prefer not to,"
And thereby affirm the one immunity
To guilt, doubt, or the deceits of circumstance.

4.

Was such the fate that mastered the orphan at last?
To have survived the mad vendetta, the whale's
Worst wrath, the suction of the sunk ship's vortex,

To end an incurable inmate in his own
Inland retreat, walled in from warring wherefores
He could not even reach to reconcile?
To learn to learn that, back of whatever masks
His mind might strike through, time was empty, and all?
Perhaps. Perhaps not quite. The fact remains
There was joy in the tale he told. The facts remained,
Inane and shapeless, their only intrinsic moral
That Waste is, has been, and may always be.
Yet, staring them down one day, might he have found
Them drawing in upon an unseen center
Which suddenly burst, releasing his own redemption?
Did hail-fellow Ishmael die indeed in the shade
Of that prison wall, of sheerest obsolescence,
That one might rise, bouyed on the old self's death,
Who'd live to know, if not a greater moral,
A greater consequence?

                       This second survivor—
I picture him, and suppose at his persuasions.
In guilt he'd again put stock, but have the passion
To call the gravest mere blank innocence:
The whale, mammal but undiscolored—a key
To its fascination and terror Ahab himself
Had never turned. Thereupon, past his own
Mind's landlocked rivers, he'd sense again the presence—
Though access be only by mountain and desert now
And no coasts visible—of the self-renewing,
Extravagant, but whimless sea through which
Pequod and crew had had to perish, laved
And sanctified by the whale's black blood. He'd sense,
Further, how in the same sea's whitest wastes
Were feeding krakens larger than Moby Dick
Whom landsmen impressed by a timeless purpose must hunt,
Hurt, and be shipwrecked by; how though the past
Give little quarter to the present, yet
Beyond neurosis still lies tragedy.

II. FROM AN ITALIAN JOURNAL: 1956-57

THE AFTER-DREAM

E quando ella fosse alquanto propinqua al salutare, uno spirito d'Amore, distruggendo tutti gli altri spiriti sensitivi, pingea fuori i deboletti spiriti del viso, e dicea loro: "Andate ad onorare la donna vostra"; ed egli si rimanea nel loco loro.

Dante, *Vita Nuova*

    Five thousand miles from her
  He dreamed of a girl he hardly knew.
Flame-flushed, she bided his approach before
The blazing fireplace of his present room,
    Tendering welcome in her less
  Than half-remembered arms and face
As though by proxy from some former love
    Sealed off at one dead self's remove.

    He woke, pleasantly thralled
  By a desire that pressed its weight
Against each hostile shadow in the cold
Pre-dawn-dim room. Through gauze drapes, street-lamp
    light
  Weighed back from the remains of last
Night's unsuccessful fire—thick, moist
Logs that had spurned the flame's advance and driven
  Him early to his bed's close haven.

    Then, for no better reason
  Than that he hardly knew her, pulling
The blankets high, closing his eyes, and easing
Himself supine, he lent his love as fully
    To her as love is lendable;
  But soon it had outgrown the small
Dream scene's capacity, and burst out bearing
  Him captive through the freer air.

    It bore him toward the east,
  To other wakenings that morning
Among the headlined heaps of Budapest,
And skies from front-page photos once more dawning
  On street scenes dense with suffering.

    He hovered there, till suddenly
Grief pressing and personal as a bodily need
    Gave abstract pity hue and heat.

    Then on around the world
    He rode it, day through dusk through evening,
On such itinerary as occurred
In the week's graver news; and he conceived
    Some estimation of the range
    And simultaneity of pain
Before he dropped through night upon a still
    House whose each feature was familiar.

    There, by those closest kin
    And claims it set him down, to lie
For warmth against their sleeping forms, with chronic
Deficiencies of sympathy supplied.
    Racked by his journey, he sank back
    Through years to where he could relax
In rich revival of a childhood fret
    Soothed by great quilts in his parents' bed.

    Lastly, it briefly took
    Him some miles further north, to picture
In sleep the girl he'd dreamed of; but her looks
Escaped, and what *she* dreamed lay past conjecture.
    Just then, light bore down on his eyes
    And forced them open on a sky
Where stars from times before his birth had been
    Extinguished by the risen sun.

            Rome, November, 1956

WITH A CAMERA IN TAORMINA

Cypress in front of flowering almond tree
   Before a silhouette of Etna,
      Against the well-proved threat
Paired as a bulwark; then, vistas of sea
      Beyond both sloping corners;
   And over all, this winter morning
Brighter than northern Junes: thus it must be.

The lower, pink-round almond has to stand
   Close in yet clear behind the cypress,
      Boughs fringing either side,
Bride to its upright, evergreen command.
      So matched, and centered, they
   Would seem to outface the volcano,
And set rapport between the sea and land.

But I have looked all morning, up and down
   The open heights of Taormina,
      And failed to find that scene,
Though all its parts show amply through the town.
      So. Be my praise for those then,
   And days when one must cull, compose,
And frame such facts to pose a paragon.

TRAFFIC ACCIDENT ON THE VIA NAZIONALE

A screech from the source of fury pierces
The heat and normal noise of noon.
"Dio," a man's voice prays or curses
Behind you, and echoes through your own
Stirred solitude. The crowd moves in.
A car on a turning hooked the wheel
Of a motorbike with its bumper, pinned
The rider under the sidelong spill,
And dragged him half a block. A cop
Cradles the half-stripped, bleeding body
Past you, head limp and mouth agape.
Some lady tourist murmurs "God."
And you, still fresh from painted Passion
And Pietà, your stomach queasy
With not quite pity though more than revulsion,
Resist the freak analogies,
Yet vibrate "God." The crowd breaks up.
Out of that moment's focus you move
Diehard again, on your interrupted
Lifetime's retreat from this after love.

TRISTANO ED ISOTTA

(*After a splendid performance of the opera at the* Maggio Musicale *in Florence, May, 1957*)

Damning *Il Wagner* for an egotistic
Teutonic barbarian of a proto-Fascist
And Decadent Romanticism's brashest
Pretender, *Dottore di Arno, Umanista,*
Consented, out of good manners, to immolate
Ear, eye, and intellect in that absurd,
Pretentious travesty of the Cornish lord
And Irish virgin potioned out of hate
To superhuman ardor. When his will
Succumbed, drugged into reverence for five
Bound hours, he blamed it on music's privative
Perils, and damned all music for his fall.

Ma, good *Dottore,* what is to be done?
Bewitched you were, through all your stout defenses?
When all one's principles abhor one's senses
Adore, does one's soul cease to be one's own?

Mah! It's no common potion *this* wizard brews.
How subtly the ceaseless modulations break
The will's resistance—whet but will not slake
Its thirst for tonic recourse and repose,
Till, weak with want, it yields its hard-held ethos.
No amenities here; no simple, clean refrain
To garner for the whistling; no humane
Italian high-jinks or domestic pathos:
Only such qualmless hastelessness as gods
Or the hubristic vaunt their power by—
From the first 'cello leap through that slow cry
Which lifts the fat, gauche singers from what clods
They may be, to knight and princess of our lulled
Credulities, patrons of our unsurer
Troths; to that final resolved *appoggiatura,*
In whose calm every woman is Iseult,
And, adolescent fantasies unshammed,
All men are Tristan, no one need be Mark,
Love is death, death love, that is all our dark
Wills know, and with *Il Wagner* we are damned.

ODE

The whole moon through a lucid
October twilight lit
A very wrinkled, lame,
Black-bonneted old woman
Toward Vespers in the round
Church of Sant'Angelo,
Fit to a low, flat hill
Snugged by Perugia's walls.
I have walked here because
A book said that this church
Would interest me. It does.
Leaves on a tree whose name
I don't know but must learn,
Coaxed by the merest breeze,
Trill, *pianissimo*.
I write this in the churchyard,
By the same light that showed,
Limping, that lady here.
She's inside now, God knows
What seeing, while I sit,
Drawn up and totally
Becalmed, outdoors, knowing
Little but that this moisture
Of summer's wane passed briefly
Across her form's alembic
Is reaching toward some root
Of me and weeding so
Well, it's beside all points
That I'm not nearly Christian.
Another day I may
Enter that church, admire
Its good fifth century
Interior, and leave
Somewhat the better for it.
Now I must wait till dark
Or a cold breeze break through
My credence, hoping hard
Her passing may be one

Of those potlucky presents
That by some cause as yet
Unanalyzed and solemn,
One often will recall.

THE TRAMS OF ROME

1.

Porta Maggiore, Rome. From one-forty-five to two,
A.M., Our Time, across the broad piazza parade
The passengerless trams, bent on the car-barns back
Of the twin white travertine arch commanding the southeast horizon.
A single light in front, guide, herald, and warning, one
By one the creaking, rattling, rectangular curios enter,
Resolve the intricate rail-maze, slip through the arch, slant off,
And disappear. In each, lit up among the leavings,
Conductor and driver, like spectres in charge of a ghost-ship, pass
From dark into dark.

                    I call to mind, as a boy in New York,
The year the city removed the trams from my borough. (*We*
Called them streetcars; "trolley" was small-town; foreigners only said "tram.")
A boy on my block, who rarely rode one inside, preferring
To hitch on the bumper to save the nickel and savor the challenge,
Called it "a crime," and vowed he'd never set foot on the brand
New bumperless buses they put in their place. He kept his vow
For close to a month, and then gave in. On some of the streets
The tracks stand yet, a source of wonder to younger children,
To most adults a driving hazard in slippery weather.

2.

Claudius Caesar, stammering cripple and posthumous god,
Who governed with something like wisdom for fourteen years until poisoned,
Had the arch built—prize link in his aqueduct stretched to the springs
Of the cordial neighboring hills. Two centuries later Aurelian,
Crude soldier and son of a peasant, who reigned four years, reformed
And protected a dissolute state, and likewise was murdered (though, times

Having changed, not deified), turned it to principal gate in
   the wall
Then needed to fortify Rome against the barbarian menace.
Thanks to the Goths, the aqueduct now is a picturesque ruin;
And Rome has outgrown such feats as its wall.

                                              With what an air
Of wonted communion they clatter by, all bearing the badge
Of their personal haunts like a password: Tram Eight, on
   duty all day
Through the green of the Villa Borghese; Thirteen, out of
   high Monteverde;
Eighteen, Seven, and Four, from past the great churches,
   Paolo,
Giovanni, Maria Maggiore—survivors thus far of one Duce,
One sham of an empire, the worst of all wars, two armed
   occupations,
Eleven years of tourist invasions, and, subway and bus
Notwithstanding, thousands of Romans per day—convening
   once more
To be cleansed, renewed, made fit for another dawn-sum-
   moned sally.

3.

The procession is done now, and Porta Maggiore relapses
   to silence.
Augmented by shadow, the arch rears nobler than lifesize
   above
The deserted piazza. But presently, dim on a distant cross-
   roads,
A point of light appears . . . intensifies . . . expands . . .
Till again the travertine gleams in the path of a tram's ap-
   proach.
A straggler? No. For look how it suddenly veers from the
   arch
And makes direct for the street-sign I stand at! *Servizio
   Notturno,*
The sign proclaims, and half of the benches are filled. I
   mount,
Pay my fare, and lurch away toward the place where I
   shall sleep.

ROMAN FAREWELL

    Dryly, as though mercifully drained
Of wants inapropos to parting, our
Lips touched and untouched. Her hand dropped my hand,
And one *Go* signal later, traffic devoured
Her form like a Death's horde sent to adjourn
Granted but deadlined colloquy between
Earth-guest and shade. I turned,
Persona non plus grata, from what had been
As precious as impossible—flush, toe
To gullet of that fact, mouthing my strong
Foretaste of last farewells—, and headlong through
The thronged square headed for the one among
Rome's tenants I knew could condole with me,
Out of his starker knowledge of what cannot be.

    Lyreless, past the dim crowds on the Corso,
Toward the high Capitol's Saturday night
Illuminations, bearing my fresh loss
As sole credential, I walked, eyes fixed straight:
Past the Horse Tamers and Philosopher King
(Small solace both), unmarked by the well-soused
River God, up museum
Stairs to that felled Gaul, staring his courage out
At the cold ground on which tired thigh and hand
Lean hard—or through it to where, nearly shade,
The thin, clean slit below the right breast and
The wrinkled marble simulating blood
Consign him—with those grim eyes that admit,
In the full starkness of their knowledge: this is it.

A BIRTHDAY CARD TO MYSELF
(October, 1956)

Between the devil on your right,
Stalking the past-dense wilderness,
Matching your pace just out of sight,
Part double, part antithesis;
And on your left, seen dizzily
Below the constant precipice,
The deep blue surface of that sea
Whose bottom may be bottomless,
For twenty-seven years now, you
Have girded growing loins to climb
This narrow rising passage through
The unmapped wood of your life's time.

Child, child-man, man-child, verge of man:
Impelled by inward oscillations
That hold your limits in their span,
Your journey through the lower stations
Of such a cross as youth could bear
Draws with its full-grown burden to
This turning point of now and here,
This steepening problem that is you.
Man, man-child, child-man, verge of child:
Far as it sees, no backward view
Can keep all data reconciled
In the vexed problem: what are you?

The one sure pattern is the chain
Of oscillations: heights, recessions;
Givings, misgivings; freshly fain
Desires to post-coital depressions;
Nocturnal fits of clarity
To dispossessed awakenings. . . .
As back and forth incessantly,
Super to sub, the pattern swings,
Where is the soul? Aloof past both
Extremes? Or stabilized between,
Taking and leaving as its growth
Demands, itself the abstract mean?

Or is it the full mongrel sum
Of every action and reaction,
Each going-to or coming-from
Evolving by another fraction

Its final form? If so, its want
Is the heart's want, and solitude
Of the forced sort can twist or stunt
It like the heart. For given good
So craves grist for its energies
That, rationed to our own reflection,
We'll knead our worst infirmities
Till loathing leavens to affection.

The problem mounts with you, must grow
As you grow. But whatever be
The soul, that self time lets you know,
Reared on this ridge between deep-sea
And devil, crossed by guilt and doubt,
Clings to the trust that two is more
Than one plus one, and seeks without
Some dearness to enhance it for
Its upward trek and the abrupt
Or sloped descent to where a new
Aloneness claims it, and the stripped
Soul stands described. I'll pray for you.

III. WEATHERS, WITHOUT AND WITHIN

MEDITATION ON THE BEACH IN PROVINCETOWN

1.

Under the clinical glare of a six A.M. sky,
Low tide weighs on the view as a guilt on the heart.
The sunken strand, stripped of its glib façade,
Exposes innards in all their literal
Uncharm—logs seaweed-pasted, random rocks,
And the occasional corpse of crustacean or fish,
Spotted through a monotony of mud.
Even the punctual gulls have forsaken the bay.
No breeze nor bird-sound varies the mass of the air
Pressing each crease and crevice into this one
Visible corner of a sea's extent.

I stare estranged, to whom last night this beach
Was resting place and plaything. Sifting sand
Through tingling fingers as loud waves broke near
And still had space to wet before the full,
I, human, felt familiar lord and master;
So brimmed with being, were that very sand
Composed of countless crumbled skeletons
And dust from dead men's brains, I should have known
Dominion. No such knowledge sounds me now.
I, human, now am alien. Overnight
An affluence has ebbed from shore and will.

2.

A woman who has lived here twenty years
Told me, for those enclosed on three sides by sea,
All rudimentaries—birth, love, and death—
Take context from the cadence of the tide.
Both children stuck in her womb awaiting the turn;
Passion was highest at high; and dying men
Were known to linger just until the ebb.
Other things equal, a native like her could tell
The lay of the water without even looking, except
At the mood she was in. And she was a sensible woman.

"Virtue is Love to Being." The one thing worse
Than hunger without the possibility
Of food is the impossibility
Of being hungry. Sin is only pure
In the limitless lust whose object is desire.
And this is orthodox, even to such

As I who know how flushed and virginal
Desire will rise from its ashes, and they blow off
With the next strong breath of the mind's variety
Or distant ripple of returning surf.

3.

For her the tide meant flesh, meant limitation.
Saint, sinner, and gull, female or male, obey
The moon's directions by a necessity
Thicker and tighter than any solar bond.
I, on this beach, am neither damned nor graced,
But merely mortal. And she was a sensible woman.
Yet some guilts cannot yield to explanation,
And lost dominion, even one morning long,
Is still sin, mine though Adam's, hers though Eve's.

Under the clinical glare of this six A.M. sky,
In this local corner of sea called Provincetown Bay,
The static strand, turned inside out like flesh,
Is cause and emblem of the soul's condition,
Not either but both. May then these logs and rocks
And occasional corpses endure their exposure until
The appointed return of the waters over them.
May this deprived sky be patient of change.
May we consent to our humanity.

APRÈS LE DÉLUGE

For seven days the world I inhabit lay
Bound and blindfolded, while a hoodlum storm
Punched and pummeled it to a muddy pulp.
On the eighth morning my world was heard to cry Uncle,
And was found, half conscious, straining for sight of a rainbow.

O what a failure, a mess, a mish-mash the sun
First noticed sprawled in that alley of early May!
And O with what a deftness did it dab,
Anoint, and dress my world, that over each sore,
In place of a scab, might sometime form a flower.

By the ninth afternoon the world I inhabit again
Inhabited me. An avenue of elms
Ran downward from my eyes, with a great puddle
Simply evaporating, halfway home.

ELEGY DURING A CONVALESCENCE

One of those days when things go piff, go poof,
Against a universe turned music-proof
About me, rain was beating time to time,
When mention of an old man's dying came
In the late mail—an old and ill man due
To die, whose death spelled deprivation to
None living but an old, ill, childless wife
Who'd "follow soon," the note predicted. Grief
Was not required, nor was it what you'd call
Grief, or its guilty lack, that blocked up all
Free circulation of my consciousness
With questions neither moot nor meaningless
Rehearsed and re-rehearsed without will, like
Some jaded juke-box tune the mind can't shake:
"How, where, and what," nagged of a dead man's spirit
And that sick mass of me that did not merit
Thought of its own survival; so that through
The waning of the rain's toneless tattoo
In the long sodden hours till sleep-time, "how,
Where, what" translated "dead, not here, there, now
Or ever anything," until each word
Lost sense, the syllables and rain beat blurred
To one flat nonsense sound, and I awoke
Healed to true mourning as the bright dawn broke.

THE LADY AND THE PILGRIM

She walked through midnight in a tall red gown.
Down thickly strange streets, empty but for her
And him, across black lots and intersections
Blown bleary by a craze of wind, she traced
A line of redness, calm and definite,
On which, for light and destination, he
Banked hope; so followed, gaining block by block.

Just as he overtook her the wind shifted,
Its roar become a rustle, its wild swirl
The mildest stroking.

      Humbly from behind
He spoke a word of greeting. The gown shivered;
She turned, fixed on him weary eyes, and in
A small voice vaguely foreign, "Please," she said,
"Go way, don't follow me no more."

         Below
The wind's increase he heard himself say "Sorry,"
And watched her sink into a sudden dawn.

SUNSHOWER

People running for cover before a burst
Of summer rain are right as the rain itself!
Smack in the middle of afternoon, the inspired
Interruption and the full authentic response,
As though New York has lapsed into a sort of
Reality a moment or so. . . .

                         And so
I and these others stand now, in hallways, under
Awnings, somewhat wet, somewhat breathless,
Each, from the run, the surprise, the abrupt jolt
Out of our separate inertias, watching
Together the rain, saying and thinking apart
And together and delighted privately
At the saying the thinking how strange it is the sun
Should be out shining yet it pours like this
And how it is a sunshower only and soon
Will pass and how all-of-a-sudden all this was
And so on. . . .

                   And all, this moment or so, downright
As right as the rain's own loud startling fragrance!

THE BALLOON

On a flesh-pink, blown-up balloon,
Like a three-dimensional man in the moon,
My caricature you painted. Strung
From the ceiling, six days and nights I hung,
Equivalent pressures without and within
Sustaining my broad, firm, prosperous grin.
But the seventh morning we woke to find,
Fluttering limp in an all-night wind,
A tiny, shriveled, scowling foetus.
That fourth dimension will always beat us:
Without or within, something must give;
No pressures are constant by which we live.
Yet grieve not, lady, this wasn't the worst.
Think of the noise if I had burst.

LATE AFTERNOON SPRING SOUNDS
BESIDE TWO OCEANS

Abed by the open window, I listened
To California spring sounds, distant
As boyhood from the adult problem that put
  Me flat on my back to think, think out
A way out of a way leading to nowhere.

A westerly breeze over backyard flowers;
  And, from the darkening east, over
Backyard fantasia of chirp and whistle, rose
  An obligato of voices of boys
And muffled, sporadic cracks of bat on ball

Riding the waves of breeze that lulled
  Stretched nerves to heavy half-asleep, full
Of easterly recollection. New York: I
  Was fifteen, a lost, problemed boy
Given to fantasy and much alone;

But on that late spring late afternoon
  The big park ballfield was the scene:
Last of the ninth, one run behind, two out,
  Two on; a packed hush; me at bat.
The pitch—he swings—Crack and a clean line drive

Rips past the shortstop's outstretched glove—
  Two dents in the platter—the ballgame's over . . . .
I stand on first base, listening to spring
  Sounds chirp and whistle and cheer, feeling
Found, found, no need to think, think out obscure

Ways out of those ways that lead one nowhere;
  Aswell and trembling with a power
That, blown through a continent and sixteen years,
  Enters, and leaves me a calm as clear,
Fantastic, and triumphant as these tears.

SUMMER IMPROMPTU

    Here everything is moving every
  thing become fluid and flowing with this
stream as lucid as obedient toward what occult
      compulsion drawing me and all of
  summer enamoured of me and of all summer.
Each and every thing (not only tree shrub grass
      but the two public signs against
  brown barks nailed handsomely and WARNING
that Hunting and Fishing are Prohibited there) glad
      to have shed brittle solidities
  to be again diffuse and yielding before
the way this day goes by so merrily so merrily
      merrily merrilymerrily life is but
  those two full streams outside and of the
blood no longer separate but coursing together and
      laughing like a couple of gods and
  God how Lavish all this day has been the
      Grace You Grant my greeds.

AFTER HIKING UP "IMP FACE" MOUNTAIN
(New Hampshire, May, 1954)

The climb was steep enough, effort enough
To sap the substance I was used to spending
Erecting steepnesses from the waste stuff
Of a hope's recent ruin. While ascending,
Body was boss. Limbs, versed in the rebirth
    That builds on failure, strained
Up the packed plenitudes of rock and earth,
And mind, mere cargo, with each fresh height gained,
Lightened, as more and more dead-wood regret
Dissolved into the good fatigue and sweat.

The top came on unheralded in one
Clean prospect. After the long shaded grind,
A rising twist of path flashed full upon
The Presidents, massed solid white behind
Gaping green hills. For what were hours then, under
    That aspect of eternal
Winter I rested, trading self for wonder,
While their sun-vaunting size belittled vernal
Attachments and obsessions, and made clear
The fallacy of seeing things too near.

By the time dusk and hunger fell, I'd had
What could be had, and rose to discipline
With a mind re-fit for control the mad
Will of descending bodies to give in
To their inertia. And I went from where
    The Presidents were fading
From white through gray, to where the cool night air
Would give sound appetite and slumber, trading
Wonder for self along the obverse climb
Back toward the blossoming aspects of time.

A MEMENTO

That April noon of nearly rain
We needed no ritual to relate us.
When, moist as the magnolia we admired
And twice as trembling, our earnest selves
Embraced in the full sympathy
Of every green and growing thing,
They rose of a sudden clear of such need
For a brief and brilliantly chimed improvisation.
　Your touch that noon, like surest laughter,
Came from a realm beyond the borders of habit
And moved, a marvelous stranger, through mine.
　Then noon had passed and we, no less
Prodigiously perhaps, descended back
On ritual; and it, cleaned and replenished,
Provided us against the afternoon
Of actual rain, and all of a moonless evening.

ON THE YEAR'S FIRST PICNIC

Three teen-age girls giggle and bask aslant
The new-green river bank. A gray-haired man
Lolls near them, seeking past his paper views
Of leg or underwear. We also loll,
Untouching male and female. With closed eyes
You mangle clover to confetti, scatter
The bits, and sigh, from no apparent cause
But my own mirrored restiveness against
The pretense in our attitudes of ease.
The soft Saturday afternoon evokes
Associations from that primal Sabbath
When, all this landscape finished and its rule
Assumed by us, we were enjoined to rest.
Grasshoppers hop about us on the grass
In animate repose, calling our bluff.

I close my eyes too, and remember how
We talked once of those Riviera ladies
Who shamelessly pursue the sun all year,
Perfecting tans with artist's care and conscience
As though such labor were their destined task.
You justified them, less than half in jest,
With "Beauty is its own excuse for being."
But when was human beauty whole or still?
The minded body is a respiteless
Demand, no statuary vision. What
But that perpetual and perfect love
We measure by at most, might temper one
To something near the poise of Emerson's
Rhodora? What but death's first puritan
And well-kept sabbath? On the other hand,

There are those figures in the *"Primavera"*
Who so possess their landscape. Spring herself
May bend under the weight of wine and wanting,
But Hermes on the other end stands stable,
Relieves the pressure of her body's arch,
Fulfills the scene. They have a right to be there,
The way these grasshoppers or that excused
Rhodora have a right to grow on ground
That complements their need, makes balance law.

Between them and the painter's gods we lie,
Glad of the turn the weather's taken, yet
Not one nor easy being two together—
Perversely precious or preciously perverse
In that fault-finding waste of ripeness by
Which we are barred from both economies?

The man peeks and the maidens giggle. No
Harm done. You stretch, open your eyes, inquire
The time, and as I tell you it comes clear
How, even were we given lovers, sharing
Spring's well-come benison and summer's promise,
We should resist most what we most awaited,
And fall must find us incomplete as ever.
Time-sense is the malaise we share, and share
With giddy girls and lonely lechers. We
Are better off than he and just as needy,
Maturer than they and just as childishly
We follow suns until the suns go down,
And then turn home relieved to contemplate
The private Primaveras we project
Against our minds' wide technicolor screens.

RAKE'S SONG

Well since we are not built for despair,
Our parts being so obsoletely
Elastic, and since there's a fair
Chance that we'll never grow completely

Accustomed to the notion that dying
Might really be dying, or that hell
Might really be hell; and since in trying
As hard as we know how to tell

Ourselves that there is nothing wrong
With us a little love won't cure,
We have a way to make the long
Postponement easier to endure;

And since your eyes are very blue,
As eyes go, and your lips, as lips
Have gone, of a warmth and redness to
My taste; since furthermore your hips

And thighs are neither too large nor lean,
Though girdled with only nature's supports,
Whereas as much of your bust as I've seen
Hints at a whole surpassing its parts:

It seems a reasonable thing,
My sweet, for me to kiss both eyes
And then both lips; then, lingering
Before both breasts and hips and thighs

Just long enough to make quite sure
No thoughts of despair or dying or hell
Will interfere, proceed to cure
My ills, and some of yours as well.

TWO REFLECTIONS FOR NANCY
(1959)

I.

Sharing space with you makes space more real.
A slovenly inwardness left so long undusted
My window on the world, I often mistrusted
What blurs and shimmerings it framed; until,
Prying it open to disclose unguessed
At riches of color and contour lucid behind
The luminous fact of you, love turned the purblind
Solipsist to rapacious realist.
Now details obsess me. I would be taught to name
All nature's erstwhile anonymities,
Distinguish specific birds in specific trees
Like that spruce-perched white-crowned sparrow lit by the
    same
Noon sun that gilds chair, piano, and bed through the clear
Window of this apartment we've furnished and share.

II.

Sharing time with you makes time less real.
While, wed to a stale stasis, for change I lusted,
Birdcall or windsweep through barren branch I trusted—
Sound's message of seasonal flux so tallied that will—,
Yet ever reflexively, as the egotist
Trusts his own semblance in another's mind,
Obtuse to all else. But how literal, now, I find
The song's brief lasting in the thrush's breast
Or the leaf's on the wind-bent branch. They tally time
Not as duration till death but of life, and please
For the health they conserve not the infirmities
They bode. So you please, daily, when you seem
Obtuse to the dust death bodes us in the care
You take of this apartment we've rented and share.

THE OSPREY

Maine honeymooners, we moored our skiff at midday
On a mile-round, fern-forested island all
Silence and greenness, as if unlived-on ever,
Unowned, and for all we might care to pretend, undiscovered.
So, like the giants we felt in our large love's pride,
Trampling the fern like some fabulous primal woodland,
We mounted the easy slope to its summit, and there
Assumed dominion over our estate.
And lordly all ways round the view we commanded
Commanded fertile ground and lake-smooth ocean,
Clean air and the sun's temperate fire.

          Only,
A strident cry now grating against the silence
Focused one ledge we had overlooked while mounting,
And sudden there, the giant osprey's nest
And the giant osprey rising straight for our sun.
Then, minded how mother hawks in fear for their nestlings
Can claw the faces of strangers, we clutched as stones
What had looked in the fern like boulders, and wished them
  larger.
High overhead, white underwings beating her mass
Into balance, as over sea-prey she poised, casting shade
The shape of those wings, fear the shape of her fear;
Till, with a second cry and the possible feint
Of a dive, she banked off leftward and down, veered back,
And set bent watching beak and unsheathed claws
In orbit round and around the exposed sun's disc,
Not twenty-five feet from our eyes.

        Round and around then
She traced that precise and dizzying ellipse,
Each full turn toward us reminded to cry that cry,
Which seemed now threat, now threnody, and touched
No less than it terrified depths of our baffled good will.
And oh how we craved some language to parley motives:
How might she teach us what gesture could put her at peace;
Or we teach her how we knew all about her nestlings,
But how there was room on this island for more than one
Large love? Or did we? Was there? What, on earth,

Not twenty-five feet from that untranslatable circling
And cry, could we begin to know of what
It is to be a bird, and in distress?

So an hour and more we suffered her suffering helpless
To help; till giddiness, aching napes, and a sun
Grown hotter than Maine suns should, strained misunder-
    standing
To critical enmity between us and the osprey;
Till only the dread of missing, or worse, just wounding,
Stayed us from flinging our stones in the teeth of that
    monstrous
Unreason, monstrously pure and exclusive love.

Then all we could do was rise, heads bent as in sign
Of our pride's abasement yet one eye fixed on the bird,
Arms loose as in proof of our peaceful intent yet a stone
Concealed in each fist, and baby-step backwards away
From the place of her nest toward the steeper and rougher
    descent
To the far side of the island. Ringed by the shadow
Of her now silent circling, we reached the rim,
Turned, dropped one stone apiece, and hand in hand,
Twice tripping on clusters of fern, went headlong within
That shadow, down and around the jagged-rocked beach
To our banishment. Over the skiff as we unmoored it,
Still silent, still too close and beyond us for comfort,
Claws, beak, and whiteness glistened round and around.
And not till we'd rowed ten lengths from the shore did she
    once
More poise, then crying one last and longest cry
Of a sense obscure as the source of her passion, break
From that orbit, show us her soaring black back, and excuse
    us.

www.ingramcontent.com/pod-product-compliance
Lightning Source LLC
Chambersburg PA
CBHW031715230426
43668CB00006B/220